6/17

DISCARD

SPORTS MATH

MATH 24/7

BANKING MATH

BUSINESS MATH

COMPUTER MATH

CULINARY MATH

FASHION MATH

GAME MATH

SHOPPING MATH

SPORTS MATH

TIME MATH

TRAVEL MATH

MATH 24/7

SPORTS MATH

RAE SIMONS

Mason Crest

Mason Crest
450 Parkway Drive, Suite D
Broomall, PA 19008
www.masoncrest.com

Printed in the United States of America.

First printing
9 8 7 6 5 4 3 2 1

Series ISBN: 978-1-4222-2901-9
ISBN: 978-1-4222-2909-5
ebook ISBN: 978-1-4222-8920-4

Cataloging-in-Publication Data on file with the Library of Congress.

Produced by Vestal Creative Services.
www.vestalcreative.com

Contents

INTRODUCTION

How would you define math? It's not as easy as you might think. We know math has to do with numbers. We often think of it as a part, if not the basis, for the sciences, especially natural science, engineering, and medicine. When we think of math, most of us imagine equations and blackboards, formulas and textbooks.

But math is actually far bigger than that. Think about examples like Polykleitos, the fifth-century Greek sculptor, who used math to sculpt the "perfect" male nude. Or remember Leonardo da Vinci? He used geometry—what he called "golden rectangles," rectangles whose dimensions were visually pleasing—to create his famous *Mona Lisa*.

Math and art? Yes, exactly! Mathematics is essential to disciplines as diverse as medicine and the fine arts. Counting, calculation, measurement, and the study of shapes and the motions of physical objects: all these are woven into music and games, science and architecture. In fact, math developed out of everyday necessity, as a way to talk about the world around us. Math gives us a way to perceive the real world—and then allows us to manipulate the world in practical ways.

For example, as soon as two people come together to build something, they need a language to talk about the materials they'll be working with and the object that they would like to build. Imagine trying to build something—anything—without a ruler, without any way of telling someone else a measurement, or even without being able to communicate what the thing will look like when it's done!

The truth is: We use math every day, even when we don't realize that we are. We use it when we go shopping, when we play sports, when we look at the clock, when we travel, when we run a business, and even when we cook. Whether we realize it or not, we use it in countless other ordinary activities as well. Math is pretty much a 24/7 activity!

And yet lots of us think we hate math. We imagine math as the practice of dusty, old college professors writing out calculations endlessly. We have this idea in our heads that math has nothing to do with real life, and we tell ourselves that it's something we don't need to worry about outside of math class, out there in the real world.

But here's the reality: Math helps us do better in many areas of life. Adults who don't understand basic math applications run into lots of problems. The Federal Reserve, for example, found that people who went bankrupt had an average of one and a half times more debt than their income—in other words, if they were making $24,000 per year, they had an average debt of $36,000. There's a basic subtraction problem there that should have told them they were in trouble long before they had to file for bankruptcy!

As an adult, your career—whatever it is—will depend in part on your ability to calculate mathematically. Without math skills, you won't be able to become a scientist or a nurse, an engineer or a computer specialist. You won't be able to get a business degree—or work as a waitress, a construction worker, or at a checkout counter.

Every kind of sport requires math too. From scoring to strategy, you need to understand math—so whether you want to watch a football game on television or become a first-class athlete yourself, math skills will improve your experience.

And then there's the world of computers. All businesses today—from farmers to factories, from restaurants to hair salons—have at least one computer. Gigabytes, data, spreadsheets, and programming all require math comprehension. Sure, there are a lot of automated math functions you can use on your computer, but you need to be able to understand how to use them, and you need to be able to understand the results.

This kind of math is a skill we realize we need only when we are in a situation where we are required to do a quick calculation. Then we sometimes end up scratching our heads, not quite sure how to apply the math we learned in school to the real-life scenario. The books in this series will give you practice applying math to real-life situations, so that you can be ahead of the game. They'll get you started—but to learn more, you'll have to pay attention in math class and do your homework. There's no way around that.

But for the rest of your life—pretty much 24/7—you'll be glad you did!

1
BASEBALL: BATTING AVERAGES

Jay loves sports. He plays several sports at his school, during the fall, winter, and spring. Plus, he follows as many sports as he can on TV, online, and in the newspapers.

One of the sports Jay pays the most attention to is baseball. Jay also happens to love math, and baseball has a lot to do with math. Fans and professionals keep track of statistics, talk about how good players are in terms of numbers, and predict what will happen in games using math.

One of the numbers used in baseball is batting average. Batting average is a number that measures how often a batter gets a base hit. Batters who strike out all the time don't have very good batting averages. Batters who hit the ball often and get to base (singles, doubles, triples, or homeruns) will have a higher batting average. Only hits that get a batter to a base count. Look on the next page to find out how to calculate batting average.

Batting averages look like this: .320, .245, .222. They are really percentages, given in decimal form.

To understand the percent form of batting averages, just move the decimal point two places to the right. That gives you the percent of times a player gets a base hit when he is at bat. So someone with a .320 batting average hits the ball 32% of the time. Someone with a .245 batting average hits the ball 24.5% of the time.

1. What are the percent forms of the following batting averages?

    .198 =
    .304 =
    .271 =
    .336 =

The formula for calculating batting average is:

$$\text{batting average} = \text{number of hits} \div \text{number of at bats}$$

If a player has 30 at bats, and he gets a base hit 9 times, his batting average would be:

$$9 \text{ hits} \div 30 \text{ at bats} = 0.300$$

There are always three numbers in a batting average, so you always have to write your calculations of batting average up to the thousandths place (the third place to the right of the decimal).

2. What is the batting average last season for Jay's favorite player if he has gotten 175 hits in 540 at bats?

You can also figure out how many hits a batter has gotten if you know his batting average and how many times he has been at bat. You just need to rearrange the equation a little:

$$\text{number of hits} = \text{batting average} \times \text{number of at bats}$$

3. If a player has a batting average of .322 and has been at bat 183 times, how many hits has he gotten?

In modern-day baseball, players almost never have batting averages that are above .400. Batting averages below .200 are considered poor.

4. If a player has 77 hits in 353 at bats, does he fall within this range? What is his batting average?

2
BASEBALL: EARNED RUN AVERAGES

While watching baseball on TV, Jay particularly likes to pay attention to the pitchers. He used to be a pitcher when he played Little League baseball when he was younger, and he likes to be the pitcher when he is playing baseball with his friends.

While batting average tells Jay how good batters are, Earned Run Average (ERA) tells him how good pitchers are. ERA is a measure of how many runs a pitcher gives up to the other team. The lower an ERA is, the better the pitcher is, because it means a pitcher didn't allow the other team to score many runs. You'll find out how to use and calculate ERA on the next page.

To calculate a pitcher's ERA for one game, add up all the innings he pitched. Pitchers don't usually pitch for the whole game, so he may have pitched for 2, 5, or 8 innings. Include parts of innings. If a player pitched one-third of an inning, add .33. If he pitched 2/3 of an inning, add .67.

Now add up all the runs the other team got in those innings, which are the pitcher's earned runs. Multiply the earned runs by 9.

Finally, divide that number by the number of innings the pitcher pitched. Make sure there are only two numbers after the decimal point. The whole equation looks like this:

$$ERA = (\text{earned runs} \times 9) \div \text{innings pitched}$$

1. What would be the ERA of a pitcher who pitched 5 innings in a game, and gave up 2 runs?

You can do the same thing to find the ERA of pitchers over a whole season, or over a player's career. You just use bigger numbers.

2. Last season, a pitcher pitched in 325 innings. He gave up 89 runs. What was his ERA?

Like with batting average, you can rearrange the ERA equation to find missing information. For example, if you know a pitcher's ERA and how many innings he played, you can find out how about many runs he gave up.

3. How many runs did a pitcher give up last month if he played 56.67 innings, and had an ERA of 4.20? The number of earned runs has to be a whole number.

   Earned runs = (ERA x innings pitched) ÷ 9
   Earned runs = (4.20 x 56.67) ÷ 9
   Earned runs =

An ERA under 2.00 is amazing. An ERA over 5.00 is poor and shows the pitcher is struggling.

4. Here are several ERAs: 3.78, 4.89, 1.93, 2.55, 5.09. Order the ERAs from least talented to most talented:

3

BASEBALL: SCORING

When Jay goes to baseball games, he likes to fill out a scorecard. He can see the score on the scoreboard, but he wants to understand how the teams get their scores.

A lot of numbers are used to score baseball. There are 3 strikes in an out and 4 balls in a walk. There are 3 outs in an inning, and 9 innings in a game. There are singles, doubles, triples, and homeruns. Hitting a single gets a player to first base. If any other players are on base, they advance one base as well. Hitting a double gets the player to second base and advances other players one or two bases, depending on how far they can get. Hitting a triple gets the player to third base and advances other players at least one base. And hitting a homerun gets the player all the way home, as well as any other players on base!

Jay finds filing out a scorecard makes it easier to keep track of all those numbers! On the next page, you'll figure out how to score a game yourself.

Here is an overview of everything that happened to Jay's favorite team in the most recent game Jay watched:

1st inning: Player 1—3 strikes; Player 2—single; Player 3—3 strikes; Player 4—double (Player 2 advances two bases); Player 5—single (Player 2 advances to home, Player 4 out at second base)

2nd inning: Player 1—fly out; Player 2—4 balls; Player 3—3 strikes; Player 4—3 strikes

3rd inning: Player 1—3 strikes; Player 2—fly out; Player 3—home run; Player 4—fly out

4th inning: Player 1—4 balls; Player 2—single (Player 1 advances one base); Player 3—single (Player 1 advances 1 base, Player 2 advances 1 base); Player 4—double (Player 1 advances home, Player 2 out at third base, Player 3 out at second base); Player 5—3 strikes

5th inning: Player 1—single; Player 2—fly out; Player 3—3 strikes: Player 4—3 strikes

6th inning: Player 1—3 strikes; Player 2—double; Player 3—3 strikes; Player 4—single (Player 2 advances to third base); Player 5—fly out

7th inning: Player 1—3 strikes; Player 2—3 strikes; Player 3—3 strikes

8th inning: Player 1-fly out; Player 2—fly out; Player 3—double; Player 4—3 strikes

9th inning: Player 1—3 strikes; Player 2—home run; Player 3—single; Player 4—fly out

1. How many strikeouts were there?

2. How many walks were there?

3. How many times did a player safely get to third base or farther?

4. What was the final score? If the other team had 3 points, did Jay's team win or lose?

4
BASKETBALL: AVERAGE HEIGHT

Jay also likes basketball. He likes to watch it on TV and go to games when he can. He plays basketball with his friends whenever he can.

Jay has never played basketball at school, though, mostly because he isn't tall enough. Basketball players tend to be really tall, so they can more easily reach the basket. You don't have to be tall to enjoy playing basketball, or even be good at it, but coaches usually want tall players.

College and professional basketball players—both women and men—are often really tall. Calculate different height averages on the next page, including mean, median, and mode.

Here are the heights on the 2012 roster for the Seattle Storm, two-time WNBA champions:

6'2" (74 inches)
5'9" (69 inches)
5'10" (70 inches)
6'6" (78 inches)
6'3" (75 inches)
6'2" (74 inches)
5'11" (71 inches)
6'2" (74 inches)
6'2" (74 inches)
6'4" (76 inches)
5'11" (71 inches)

The average most people are used to talking about is called the mean. You need to add up all the heights and then divide by the number of heights you added. It's easiest to calculate the mean just in inches, and then convert to feet and inches.

1. What is the mean of their heights in inches? Round to the nearest whole inch. What is that in feet and inches?

The median is another average. Arrange the heights in order from least to greatest. Then cross off the shortest and tallest players. Keep doing that until you arrive at one number in the middle. If there are two numbers, you can take the mean of them to find the number that is exactly in the middle.

2. What is the median for these heights?

A third kind of average is called the mode. The mode is the height that occurs the most.

3. What is the mode?

4. If the average height for women in the United States is around 5'4", how many inches taller is the average women on the Seattle Storm?

5
BASKETBALL: WIN-LOSS

During basketball season, Jay likes to follow every team in the college and professional leagues. He checks online for the teams' **standings** every week. The number he looks at is the win-loss number. When he sees a number like 9–3, he knows that team won 9 games and lost 3. They played a total of 12 games.

Another number that goes along with win-loss is win percentage. Win percentage is a measure of how many games a team has won compared to how many they have played. Then you can take a look at every team's win percentage, and you can tell which teams have played the best during a season so far. The next page will help you practice understanding win-loss and win percentages.

Jay takes a look at the win-loss numbers for several basketball teams midway through the season. He sees:

4–10
14–1
5–10
9–5
7–7
3–12
1–13

1. Which team has a better win-loss record, the team with 1–13 or the team with 14–1?

2. How many games have those two teams played?

You can see some of the teams have played different numbers of games, so comparing them to each other gets a little tricky. To figure out just how well each team has done in comparison to the other teams, you'll need to find the win percentage. The formula is:

win percentage = wins ÷ total games played.

In basketball, win percentage is usually shown as a decimal number, with three decimal places. To convert to a normal percent, just move the decimal point two places to the left.

3. What is the win percentage for the 1–13 team and the 14–1 team? Give your answers in both decimal and percent form.

4. Now you can order the teams from first to last, starting with the team with the highest win percentage (a) and ending with the team with the lowest (g).

   a.
   b.
   c.
   d.
   e.
   f.
   g.

6
FOOTBALL: SCORING

Another sport Jay likes is football. He watches games on TV, plays for fun with his friends on the weekend, and even plays on his school's team. He dreams about becoming a professional football player in the future.

Football, like other sports, has a lot of numbers and math. Anyone who watches or plays football has to learn the many different ways of scoring points. Every game is different, even if the scores end up being the same. Find out on the next page how you can combine points to get scores.

Here are the ways players score points in a football game:

a touchdown = 6 points

an extra point after a touchdown = 1 point

a 2-point conversion = 2 points

a field goal = 3 points

a safety = 2 points

In the last football game Jay played in, his high school team won with 34 points. The other team scored 29 points.

1. Jay's team scored four touchdowns. How many points did they score in other ways besides touchdowns?

2. What is one way the team could have scored those points using all four other ways of scoring?

3. What is one way the losing team could have scored 29 points if they also had four touchdowns?

4. If the other team had gotten one more touchdown, would they have won the game? Why or why not?

7
FOOTBALL: ROMAN NUMERALS

The Super Bowl is one of Jay's favorite days. He and his family all watch the Super Bowl together. They make special food and wear their team's jerseys.

In 2013, they watched the forty-seventh annual Super Bowl. However, the game isn't advertised using the normal numbers we use today in math class. Instead, the year of the Super Bowl is given in Roman numerals, so the 2013 game was Super Bowl XLVII. Jay's younger sister was a little confused about how to read Roman numerals, so Jay taught her how during the game. You'll learn too, on the next page.

In Roman numerals, different letters stand for certain numbers.

I = 1
V = 5
X = 10
L = 50
C = 100
D = 500
M = 1,000

You form numbers by adding different letters together. Two would just be two 1s, or II. Three would be three 1s, or III. But four is a little different. You don't want to list four IIIIs in a row. Instead, you write IV, which means "one less than five." You do the same thing for ten, but using an X instead of a V.

1. What is one through ten in Roman numerals?

For the forty-seventh Super Bowl, the Roman numeral is XLVII. You can divide that into different numbers you add together. Divide it by places: first look at the tens place, then the ones place.

The XL is the tens place. It really means "ten less than fifty." You might have thought XL would mean 60, because ten and fifty added together is 60. But every time you see a letter that has less value than the letter that comes after it, you subtract it instead of add it. If it were 60, it would read LX, and the ten would come after the fifty.

After XL is VII. That's just 5 plus 2, or 7. Add the XL in the tens' place and the VII in the ones' place together and you get 47.

2. What was Super Bowl forty-six in Roman numerals?

3. In 2023, it will be Super Bowl fifty-seven. What will that be in Roman numerals?

You can also give larger numbers in Roman numerals, like the year of the forty-seventh Super Bowl—2013.

4. What is 2013 in Roman numerals?

8
SOCCER: FIELD AREA

Jay's friend Ananya loves to play soccer. She is one of the star players on her school team, and she wants to become a professional soccer player someday.

Ananya and Jay's school is building a new soccer field because their old one was flooded and was really old. The new soccer field has to be built using exact measurements. The dimensions of the field are important. Soccer fields at every school and in professional games are around the same size so players get used to how big they are and what to expect. A team won't have an unfair advantage when other teams come to play on their field and aren't used to the size.

The next page will take you through soccer field dimensions, and will help you calculate the area of the field.

The new soccer field, at the school will be 100 yards long and 60 yards wide. (Remember, 1 yard equals 3 feet.)

You already have enough information to calculate the area of the field. The area of a rectangle is:

$$area = length \times width$$

1. What is the area of the field in square yards?

Now find the area in square feet. First, convert the yards into feet by multiplying each dimension by 3. Then plug those numbers into the area equation.

2. What is the area of the field in square feet?

The school also has to draw lots of lines on the field and set up the goals. The midfield line, for example, divides the field in half lengthwise, and shows which side the teams are defending.

3. How far down the length of the field (in feet) should the midfield line be drawn?

What is the area of each half of the field in square feet?

On either end of the field, in front of the goals, are the goal areas. Players have to kick the ball from this area to score a goal.

Goal areas are 120 square yards in area. If one side of the goal area is 20 yards long, you can find the missing piece of information (the width) by rearranging the area equation.

The new equation would be:

$$width = area \div length$$

4. So, the width = 120 square yards ÷ 20 yards =

5. What is the width of the goal area in feet?

9
TENNIS: SCORING

Jay's friend Kwan plays tennis. Sometimes Jay goes and watches his tennis matches and cheers his friend on. Kwan is pretty good—he wins a lot of the time.

At first, figuring out how tennis scores work was a little confusing for Jay, because tennis doesn't just count points from 1 on up. Instead of 1, 2, 3, 4, and so on, tennis uses a different scoring system. Jay quickly figured it out, and you can too.

Here is how tennis is scored:

0 points = love
1 point = 15 game points
2 points = 30 game points
3 points = 40 game points
4 points = 60 game points/game over

And here are some of the rules of scoring one game:

- You must earn a minimum of 4 points to win a game.
- You must win by 2 points.
- If you are not ahead by 2 points by the time you get 40 game points, the next point you score is called advantage. If you get another point, you win the game.
- The score is announced server first.

In one game Jay watches Kwan play, Kwan has scored 1 point and his opponent has scored 3 points. Kwan is the one serving next.

1. What is the score in tennis terms?

Kwan's opponent scores the next point.

2. What is the score? Is the game over?

Kwan and Jay aren't too worried, though. Losing this game doesn't mean Kwan has lost the whole match. In tennis, you need to win 6 games to win one set. You also have to win by 2 games in a set.
    As the game goes on, Kwan ends up winning 5 games. His opponent wins 4.

3. What will happen in this set if Kwan wins the next game?

4. What will happen in this set if Kwan's opponent wins the next game?

Finally, tennis players usually play 3 sets in the whole match. The winner has to win two out of the three sets.
    Kwan wins one set and his opponent wins one set. They have to play one more to decide who will win the match. With one game to go, the final set is scored 5–4 in favor of Kwan.

5. Will Kwan win the match if he wins this set? Why or why not?

10
TRACK: RECORDS

Once in a while, Jay goes to a track meet at his school. He has a few friends on the team, and he likes to cheer them on.

He wonders what the world records are for track. His friends are fast, but he knows that the men and women who train to run can go a lot faster! When he gets home after a track meet, he looks up the world records for track. He can see they are really fast, but he isn't sure exactly how the times compare to his friends' times.

Putting track time data on a line graph could help Jay compare the times. You can do the same thing on the next page.

Jay decides to compare records for the men's 100-meter dash, the shortest track event. Here's the information he finds for world records in the last few years:

2009 world record: 9.58 seconds
2008 world record: 9.69 seconds
2007 world record: 9.74 seconds
2006 word record: 9.762 seconds
2005 world record: 9.768 seconds
2002 world record: 9.78 seconds
1999 world record: 9.79 seconds

And here is the data for his school for the same years:

2009 school record: 10.39
2008 school record: 10.41
2007 school record: 10.42
2006 school record: 10.56
2005 school record: 10.59
2002 school record: 10.60
1999 school record: 10.67

Now fill out the rest of this line graph, with two lines: one for the world record and one for the school record.

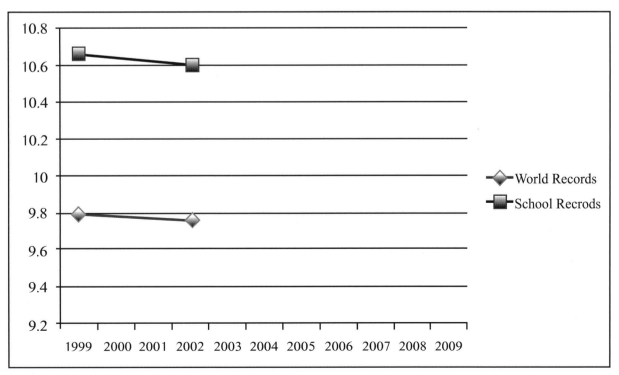

11
GOLF: PAR

J ay is flipping through the channels on his TV when he comes across golf. He hasn't really watched much golf before, but he decides he wants to learn more about how golf is played and scored.

He finds that like other sports, golf has plenty of numbers involved. In golf, players go through 18 different holes. Each hole has a par, which is the number of shots it should take to get the golf ball in the hole. Harder holes have higher pars, while easier holes have lower pars. Players win by getting the ball in the holes in as few strokes as possible.

Jay figures out the rules pretty quickly, and can tell who the best players are from their scores on individual holes. See if you can do the same on the next page.

Par is based on how difficult the hole is. Holes with higher pars are generally really long. They also may have sharp turns or hills.

1. Would a hole that is 200 yards long and straight have a higher or lower par than a hole that is 320 yards long with a curve in the middle? Why?

Golf courses often have 18 holes that add up to 72, though not always.

2. Does a course with four par-3 holes, ten par-4 holes, and four par-5 holes add up to 72?

3. Which are the most difficult holes on this golf course?

Golf has different terms for how many strokes it takes to get the ball in the holes, besides par.

double eagle: 3 strokes under par, or –3
eagle: 2 strokes under par, or –2
birdie: 1 stroke under par, or –1
par: par, or 0
bogey: one stroke over par, or +1
double bogey: two strokes over par, or +2
triple bogey: three strokes over par, or +3

The best players get birdies, eagles, or double eagles.
    To calculate a player's score, just add up the numbers associated with the number of shots above or below par it took for the player to get the ball in the hole.
    The player Jay is watching gets a par, a bogey, and an eagle on the first 3 holes.

4. What is her overall score?

The next hole is a par-5 hole. She takes 4 strokes to get the ball in the hole.

5. What is her score on this hole? What is her overall score now that she has played another hole?

12
SWIMMING:
LAPS AND DISTANCE

Jay's younger brother Leo takes swimming lessons. He wants to be on the school team eventually, but he has to practice more first. Right now, he takes lessons in a 25-yard pool. If he joins the swim team, though, he'll swim in a 50-meter pool, which is a little bigger.

Every lap Leo swims in either pool is a certain distance. Swim competitions involve different numbers of laps, which **correspond** to different distances.

Sometimes Leo has trouble remembering how many laps in the pool each distance is. These tables will help him:

25-Yard Pool
1 length = 25 yards (from wall to wall)
2 lengths = 50 yards
4 lengths = 100 yards
¼ mile = about 500 yards = 20 lengths
½ mile = about 800 yards = 32 lengths
1 mile = about 1700 yards = 68 lengths
1.2 miles = about 2000 yards = 80 lengths
2.4 miles = about 4000 yards = 160 lengths

50-Meter Pool

1 length = 50 meters
2 lengths = 100 meters
¼ mile = about 400 meters = 8 lengths
½ mile = about 800 meters = 16 lengths
1 mile = about 1500 meters = 30 lengths
1.2 miles = about 2000 meters = 40 lengths
2.4 miles = about 4000 meters = 80 lengths

1 meter = 1.0936 yards/ 1 yard = 0.9144 meters

You can use all these numbers to figure out how far Leo swims during his practices.

1. How many lengths of the pool (laps) will Leo swim if he swims 100 yards?

Leo and his classmates are doing a relay in swim class. There are 5 people per team and each of them swims 4 lengths of the 25-yard pool.

2. What distance do they all swim together?

If Leo makes it onto the school swim team, he will be swimming in a 50-meter pool, which means he will be swimming longer distances for each lap. Use the conversions between meters and yards above.

3. How long is one length of the 50-meter pool in yards? How much longer is one length of the 50-meter pool than two lengths of the 25-yard pool?

4. If Leo and his 4 friends were to do the same relay race in the 50-meter pool, what distance would they have swum if they all swam four lengths? What is that distance in yards?

13

HOCKEY: ANGLES

Jay is also on his school's hockey team. He has an **offensive** position, so he sometimes scores goals. He isn't the highest-scoring player on his team, but he'd like to be. He needs to practice more to get even better.

Math can also help Jay get better. Hockey involves a lot of angles, as Jay has found out. If he doesn't shoot the puck at the right angle when he's trying to score a goal, he won't make it. He knows it's worth it to understand angles in order to score more goals and become a better hockey player. Try out your own understanding of angles in hockey.

Here are some common angles you'll find in hockey:

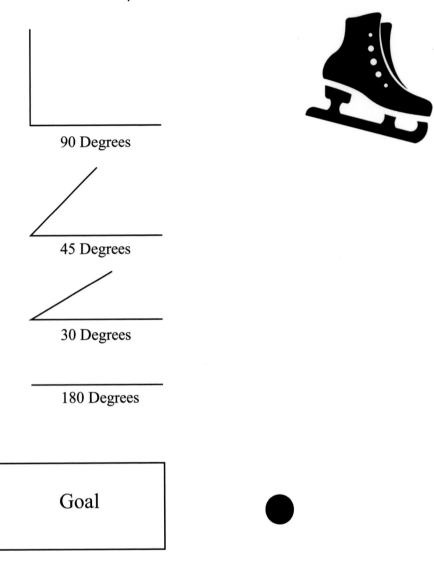

90 Degrees

45 Degrees

30 Degrees

180 Degrees

Goal

1. What angle do you estimate the puck on the far left to be from the middle of the goal?

2. What angle do you think the middle puck is from the middle of the goal?

3. And what about the puck on the right? Will the player be able to shoot it into the goal at that angle?

14
OLYMPIC MEDALS

The Olympics happen every two years, rotating between the summer and winter Olympics. Jay watches all of them, and tries to see as many sports as possible.

In 2012, London hosted the summer Olympics. After the games, people tallied up the number of medals each country had won, and compared them to each other. You can use bar graphs to easily compare different countries overall and in different sports. Graphs offer an easy way to visualize what is going on in the Olympics. Turn to the next page to fill in your own graph.

The countries that got the most medals in the 2012 Summer Olympics were:

United States: 46 gold, 29 silver, 29 bronze
China: 38 gold, 27 silver, 27 bronze
Russia: 24 gold, 26 silver, 32 bronze
Great Britain: 29 gold, 17 silver, 19 bronze
Germany: 11 gold, 19 silver, 14 bronze

1. What was the total number of medals each country won?

Finish out this bar graph of medal scores, so that you can see how each country compares. The first country has been done for you.

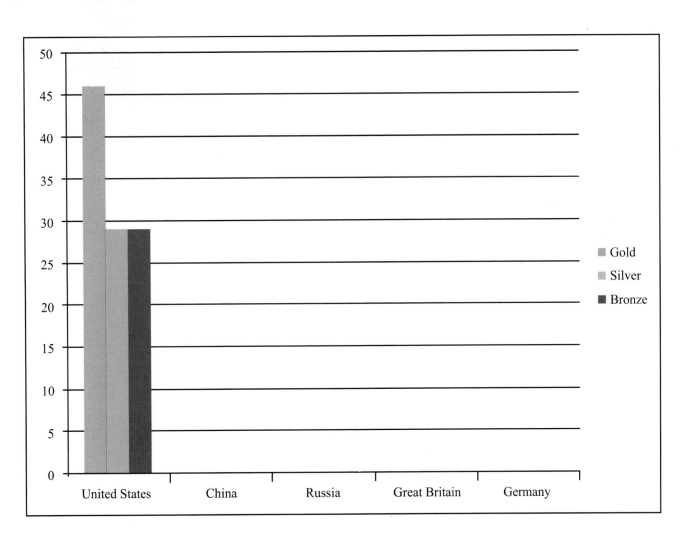

15
PUTTING IT ALL TOGETHER

Jay and his family and friends play a lot of sports. The longer he plays, the more Jay understands that math is a big part of sports. From keeping track of scores, to figuring out the area of a field, to figuring out who is the best player or team, math makes sports more fun and improves the game. On the next page, see if you can remember some of what you have learned along with Jay.

1. In one baseball game, a batter has 5 at bats. He gets a base hit twice in those 5 at bats. What is his batting average for the game?

2. A pitcher has pitched 137 ⅓ innings this baseball season so far. He has given up 39 runs during those innings. What is his ERA?

3. A basketball team wins 14 games out of the 23 games it plays. What is the team's win-loss number?

   What is the team's win percentage?

4. What Super Bowl will be played in the year 2030, in Roman numerals?

5. A soccer field's area is 6820 square yards and it is 62 yards wide. How long is the soccer field?

6. A tennis player's score during the last game of a set is 30–love (she is serving). The two players are tied in the set, 5–5 .

   How many more points does she need to win the game?

   Does winning the game mean the player wins the set? Why or why not?

7. On a par-4 hole at the golf course, a player takes 6 strokes to get the ball in the hole.

   What is his score for the hole?

8. In a 25-yard pool, how many lengths would it take to swim a mile?

   What about in a 50-meter pool?

Find Out More in Books

Adamson, Thomas Kristian. *Baseball: The Math of the Game*. North Mankato, Minn.: Capstone Press, 2011.

Adamson, Thomas Kristian. *Basketball: The Math of the Game*. North Mankato, Minn.: Capstone Press, 2011.

Frederick, Shane Gerald. *Football: The Math of the Game*. North Mankato, Minn.: Capstone Press, 2011.

Frederick, Shane Gerald. *Hockey: The Math of the Game*. North Mankato, Minn.: Capstone Press, 2011.

Tyler, Marya Washington and Kip Tyler. *Extreme Math: Real Math, Real People, Real Sports*. Waco, Tex.: Prufrock Press, Inc., 2004.

Walsh, Kieran. *Sports Math*. Vero Beach, Fla.: Rourke Publishing, 2005.

FIND OUT MORE ON THE INTERNET

Math in Sports
math2033.uark.edu/wiki/index.php/Math_In_Sports

Maths and Sports: Countdown to the Games
sport.maths.org/content/

PBS Kids: Cyberchase
www.pbskids.org/cyberchase/find-it/math-and-sports

The Science of Baseball
www.exploratorium.edu/baseball

Sports Math
classic.sidwell.edu/LS_Math_Adventures/sports.htm

GLOSSARY

Annual: something that happens every year.

Convert: to change into.

Correspond: to match or go along with.

Data: information, often in number form.

Dimensions: measurements of size, including, for example, length and width.

Estimate: to guess.

Offensive: trying to score goals, as opposed to trying to defend a goal.

Range: the area between a lower and an upper limit.

Roster: a list of active players who can be called on to play.

Standings: comparisons of how various teams are doing.

Statistics: collecting and analyzing numerical information—numbers—in large quantities.

Tallied: counted up.

Value: how much something is worth.

Visualize: to imagine as a picture, to see in your mind.

Answers

1.

1. .198 = 19.8%
   .304 = 30.4%
   .271 = 27.1%
   .336 = 33.6%
2. .324
3. 59 hits
4. Yes, he has a batting average of .218.

2.

1. $(2 \times 9) \div 5 = 3.6$
2. $(89 \times 9) \div 325 = 2.46$
3. 26
4. 5.09, 4,89, 3.78, 2.55, 1.93

3.

1. 15
2. 2
3. 5
4. They had 4 points, and won the game.

4.

1. 73 inches; 6'1"
2. 74 inches/6'2"
3. 74 inches/6'2"
4. 9 inches

5.

1. 14–1
2. 14 and 15
3. $^{0.071}/_{7.1}$%; $^{0.933}/_{93.3}$%
4. a. 14–1
   b. 9–5
   c. 7–7
   d. 5–10
   e. 4–10
   f. 3–12
   g. 1–13

6.

1. 10 points
2. One field goal, a 2-point conversion, 2 safeties, and an extra touchdown point OR 2 2-point conversions, a field goal, a safety, and an extra touchdown point. There are more answers as well.
3. One field goal and a safety, OR two safeties and a touchdown point. There are many more answers.
4. Yes, they would have had 1 more point than Jay's team.

7.

1. I, II, III, IV, V, VI, VII, VIII, IX, X
2. XLVI
3. LVII
4. MMXIII

8.

1. 6000 square yards
2. 54,000 square feet
3. 50 yards/150 feet; 27,000 square feet
4. 6 yards
5. 18 feet

9.

1. 15–40
2. 15–game, yes the game is over.
3. Kwan wins the set.
4. The score will be 6-5, and they will need to play at least one more game.
5. Yes, because he will have won it by 2 points.

10.

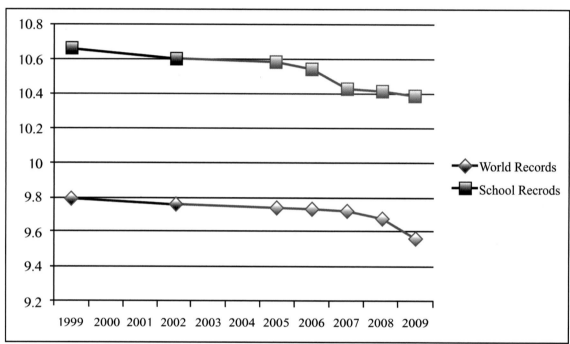

11.

1. Lower par, because it is easier to get the ball in the hole.
2. Yes
3. The par-5 holes
4. $0 + 1 - 2 = -1$
5. $-1; -2$

12.

1. 4
2. ¼ mile/500 yards
3. 50 x 1.0936 = 54.68 yards; 4.68 yards longer
4. 1000 meters; 1,093.6 yards

13.

1. 30 degrees
2. 45 degrees
3. 90 degrees; no

14.

1. US = 104, China = 92, Russia = 82, Great Britain = 65, Germany = 44

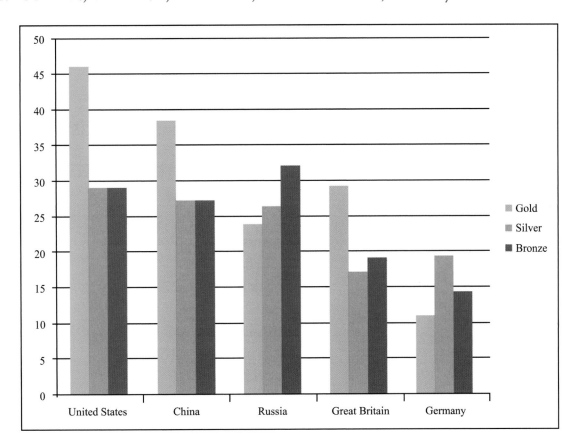

15.

1. 2 hits ÷ 5 at bats = .400
2. (39 x 9) ÷ 137.33 = 2.56
3. 14–9; 0.609/60.9%
4. LXIV
5. 6044 ÷ 62 = 97.48 yards
6. 2 more; no, she doesn't win the set, because she has to win by two games.
7. Double bogey/+2
8. 68 lengths; 30 lengths

INDEX

ABOUT THE AUTHOR

Rae Simons is a well-established educational author, who has written on a variety of topics for young adults for the past twenty years.

Picture Credits